The Holy Family

Heirloom Nativity - Book 1

by Carol Emmer

LeisureArt Inc., • Maumelle Arkansas

Table of Contents

Instructions tested and cover items made by Kandi Ashford, Marsha Besancon, Vicky Bishop, Karen Brogan, Joyce Holland, and Marie Williford.

Made in U.S.A.

DONKEY (88w x 68h)

X	DMC	¼X	½X	B'ST	JPC	COLOR
	420				5374	hazel brown
	422				5372	lt hazel brown
	640				5393	dk beige grey
	642				5832	beige grey
	644				5831	lt beige grey
	644 & 3023					lt beige grey & lt brown grey
	676				2874	lt gold
	680				2876	dk gold
	822				5830	vy lt beige grey
	869					dk yellow beige
	938				5477	vy dk brown
	3045				2412	yellow beige
	3781					dk beige brown
	3790					vy dk beige grey

DONKEY (88w x 68h)

14 count	$6\frac{3}{8}''$	x	$4\frac{7}{8}''$
16 count	$5\frac{1}{2}''$	x	$4\frac{1}{4}''$
18 count	$5''$	x	$3\frac{7}{8}''$
22 count	$4''$	x	$3\frac{1}{8}''$

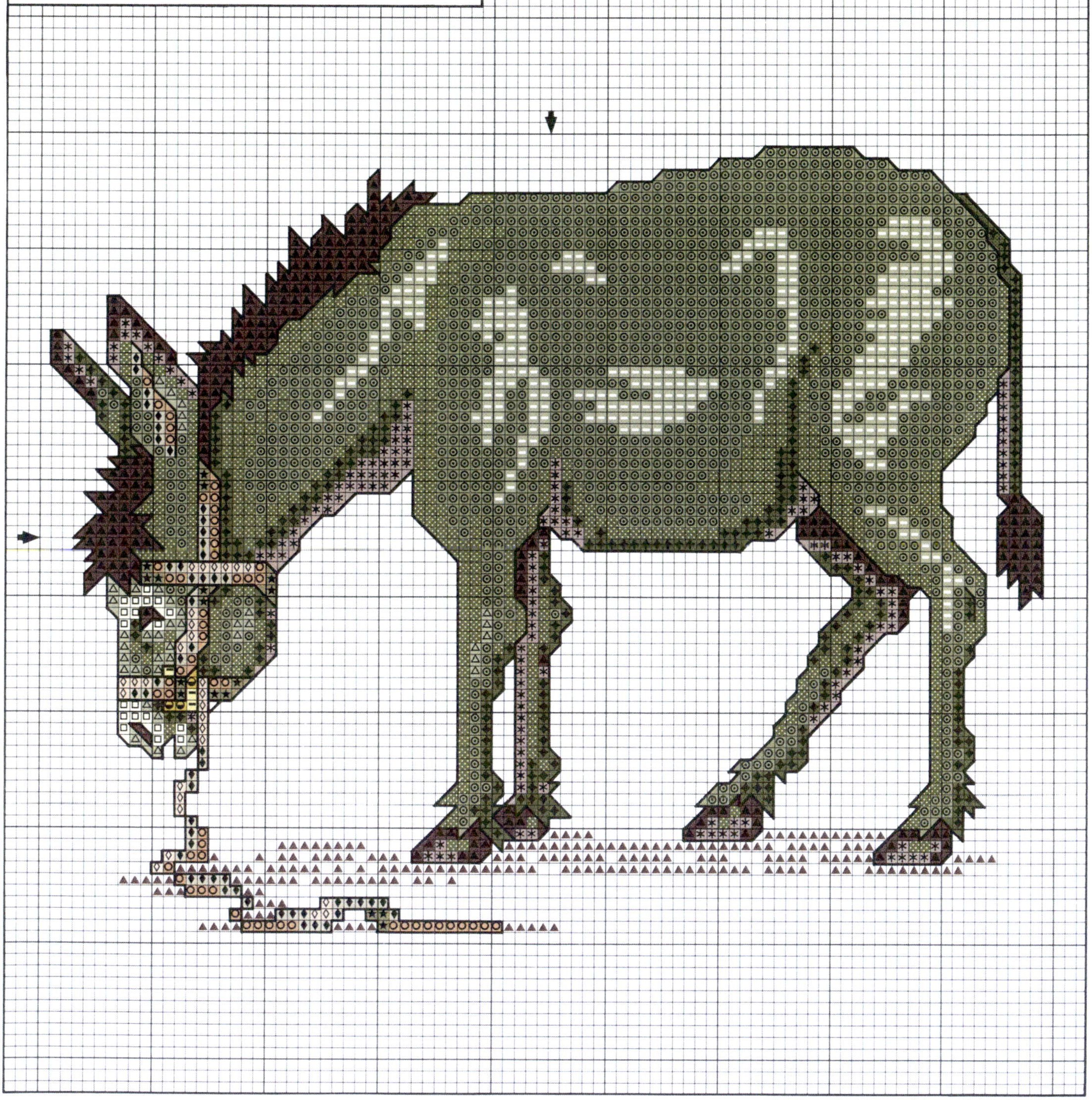

MARY (78w x 112h)			
14 count	5⅝″	x	8″
16 count	4⅞″	x	7″
18 count	4⅜″	x	6¼″
22 count	3⅝″	x	5⅛″

Color key for Mary is on page 5.

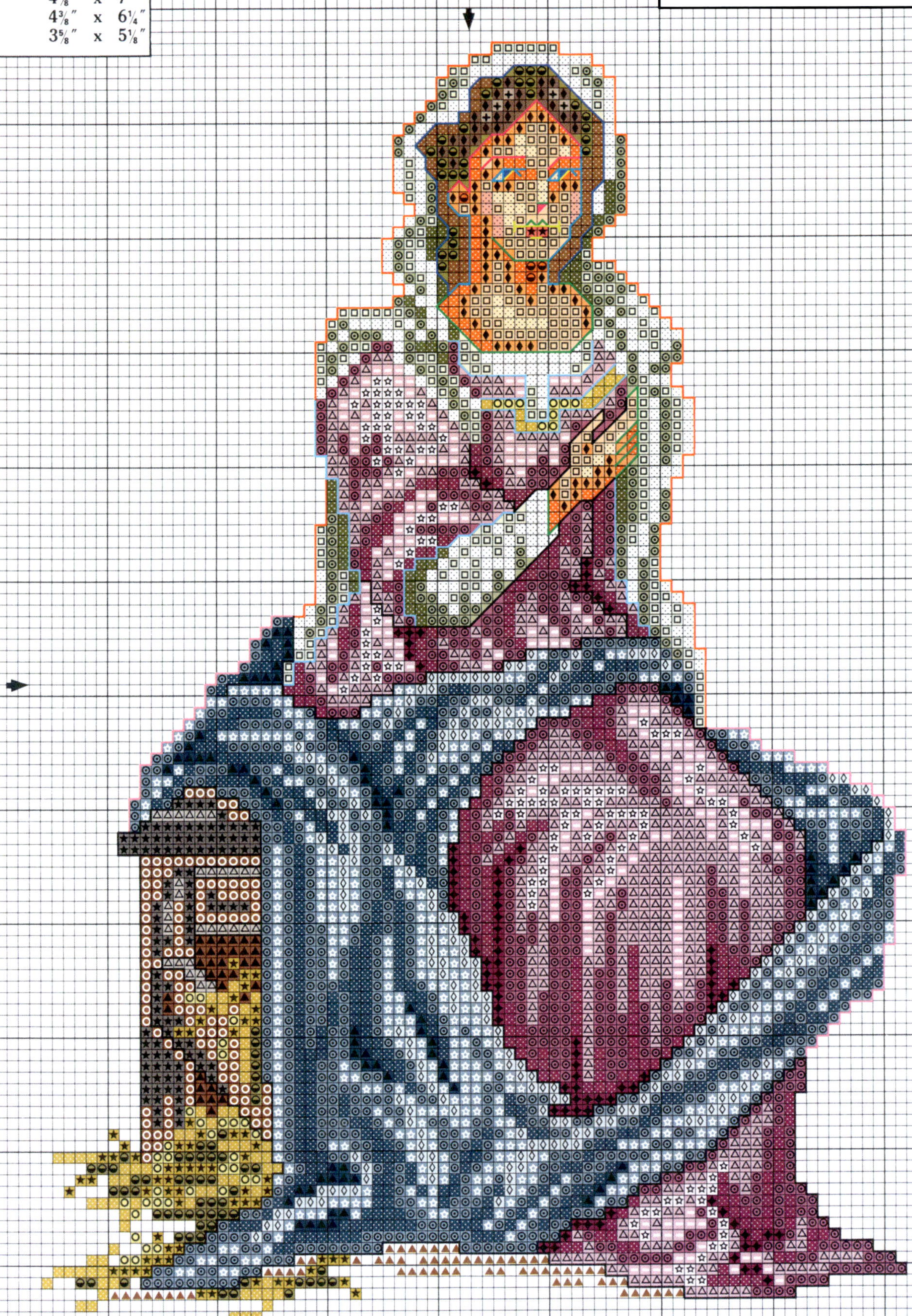

MARY (78w x 112h)
JESUS (66w x 50h)

X	DMC	¼X	¾X	B'ST	JPC	COLOR
	blanc				1001	white
	221				3242	vy dk pink
	223				3241	lt pink
	224				3240	vy lt pink
	225				3239	baby pink
	353				3006	peach
	356				2338	dk peach
	420				5374	hazel brown
	422				5372	lt hazel brown
	433				5471	lt brown
	434				5000	vy lt brown
	435				5371	tan
	640				5393	dk beige grey
	642				5832	beige grey
	644				5831	lt beige grey
	676				2874	lt gold
	677					vy lt gold
	680				2876	dk gold
	729				2875	gold
	754				2331	lt flesh
	758				3868	flesh

X	DMC	¼X	½X	B'ST	JPC	COLOR
	760				3069	salmon
	801				5475	brown
	822				5830	vy lt beige grey
	869					dk yellow beige
	924				6008	vy dk grey blue
	926				6007	grey blue
	927				6006	lt grey blue
	928				7225	vy lt grey blue
	931				7051	blue
	938				5477	vy dk brown
	948				2331	vy lt flesh
	3031				5472	dk brown
	3032				5393	lt beige brown
	3045				2412	yellow beige
	3064				3883	dk flesh
	3721					dk pink
	3722					pink
	3768					dk grey blue
	3772				5579	vy dk flesh
	3781					dk beige brown

JESUS (66w x 50h)

14 count	4¾"	x	3⅝"
16 count	4⅛"	x	3⅛"
18 count	3¾"	x	2⅞"
22 count	3"	x	2⅜"

COW (106w x 60h)					
X	DMC	¼X	½X	B'ST	JPC	COLOR
	blanc				1001	white
	300					vy dk rust
	301					rust
	400					dk rust
	640				5393	dk beige grey
	642				5832	lt beige grey
	644				5831	vy lt beige grey
	822				5830	beige
	922				3336	vy lt rust
	938				5477	vy dk brown
	3776					lt rust
	3781					beige brown
	3790					vy dk beige grey

COW (106w x 60h)			
14 count	7⅝"	x	4⅜"
16 count	6⅝"	x	3¾"
18 count	6"	x	3⅜"
22 count	4⅞"	x	2¾"

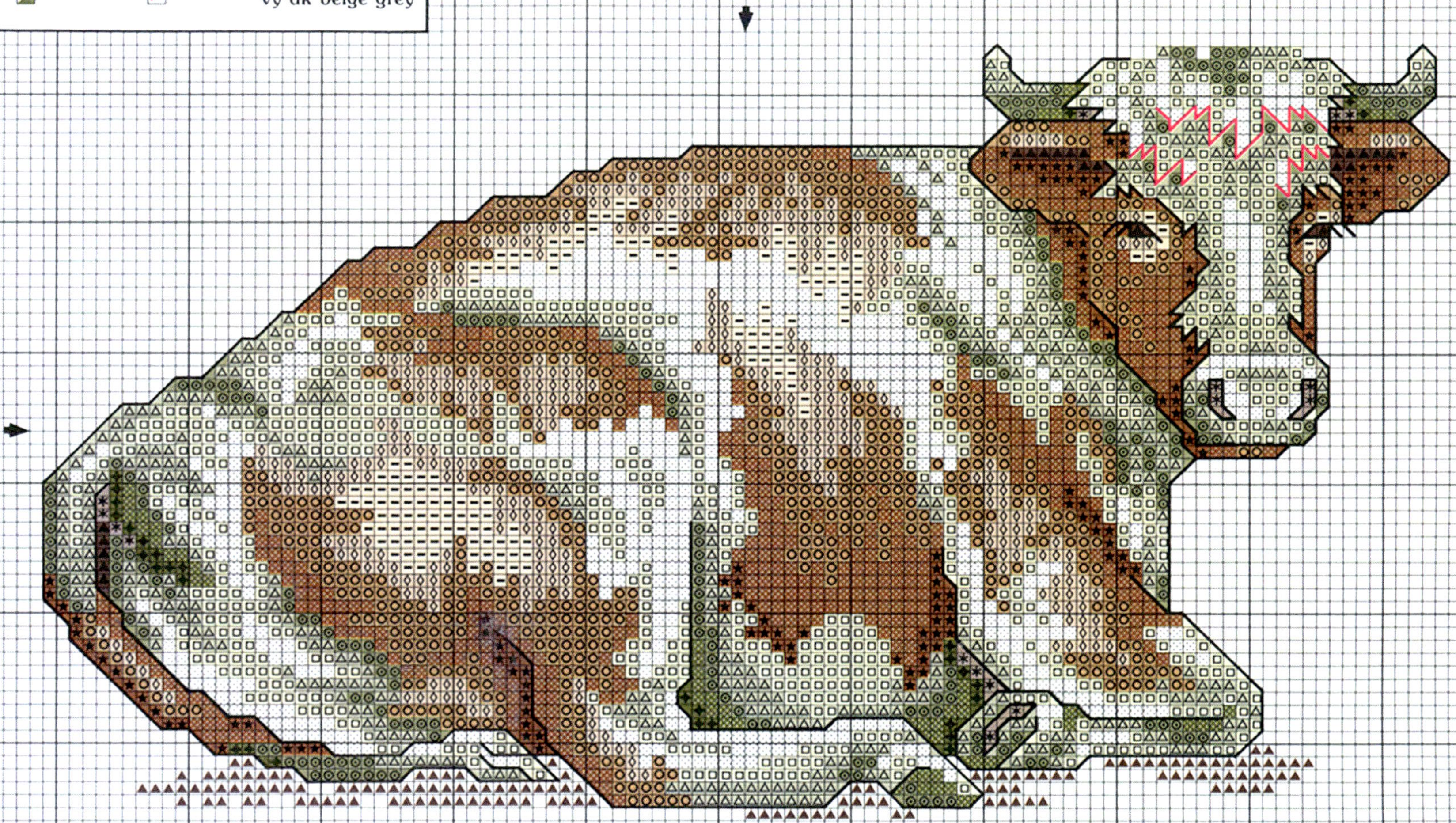

JOSEPH (62w x 119h)

X	DMC	¼X	½X	B'ST	JPC	COLOR
	blanc				1001	white
	356				2338	dk peach
	420				5374	hazel brown
	522				6316	lt green
	523				6316	vy lt green
	642				5832	beige grey
	644				5831	lt beige grey
	754				2331	lt flesh
	758				3868	flesh
	801				5475	brown
	822				5830	vy lt beige grey
	869					dk yellow beige
	931				7051	blue
	935				6270	vy dk green
	938		▲		5477	vy dk brown
	948				2331	vy lt flesh
	3021				5395	vy dk brown grey
	3022					brown grey
	3023					lt brown grey
	3024				8390	vy lt brown grey
	3031				5472	dk brown
	3045				2412	yellow beige
	3064				3883	dk flesh
	3362				6318	dk green
	3363				6317	green
	3772				5579	vy dk flesh
	3787					dk brown grey

JOSEPH (62w x 119h)			
14 count	4½"	x	8½"
16 count	3⅞"	x	7½"
18 count	3½"	x	6⅝"
22 count	2⅞"	x	5½"

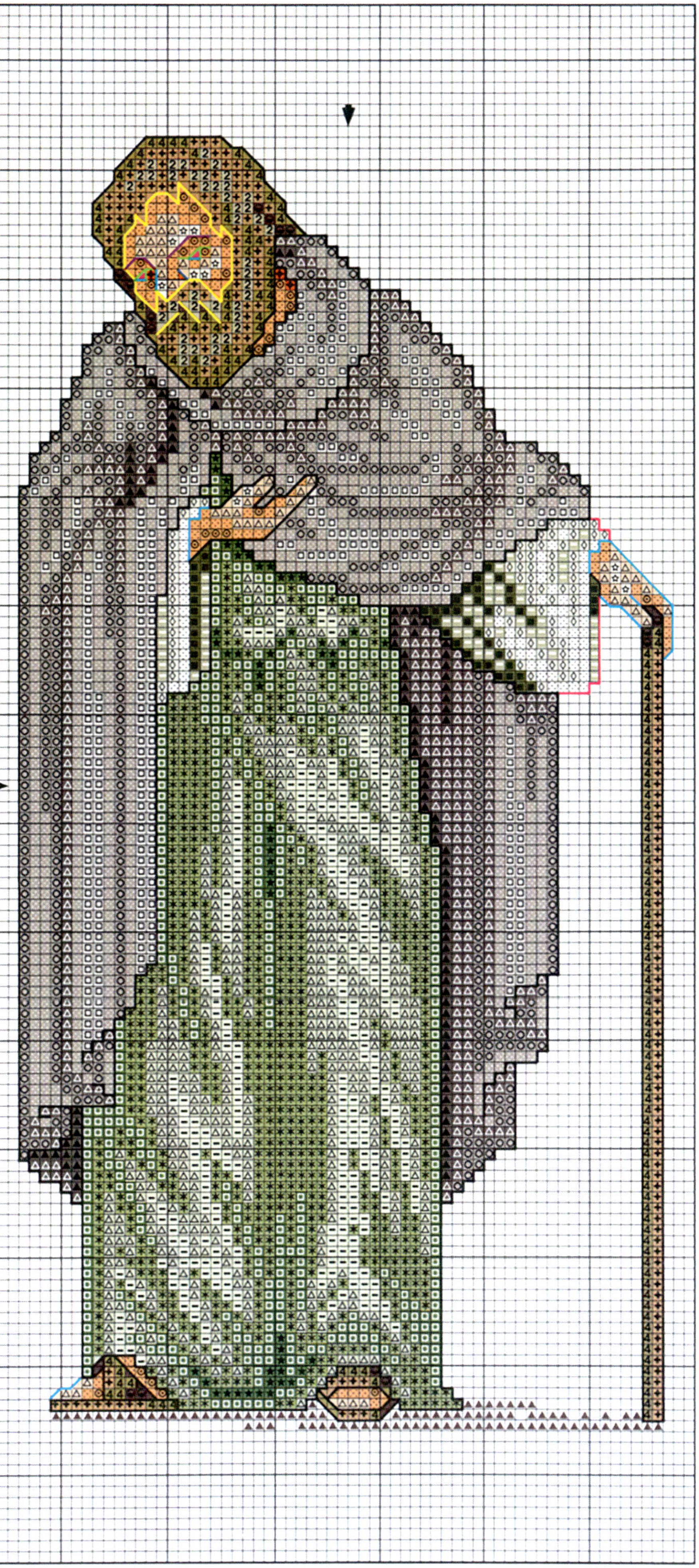

GENERAL INSTRUCTIONS

WORKING WITH CHARTS

How To Read Charts: Each of the designs is shown in chart form. Each colored square on the charts represents one Cross Stitch or one Half Cross Stitch. Each colored triangle on the charts represents one One-Quarter Stitch or one Three-Quarter Stitch. The straight lines on the charts indicate Backstitch. When a Backstitch crosses a square, the symbol is omitted.

Each chart is accompanied by a color key. This key indicates the color of floss to use for each stitch on the chart. The headings on the color key are for Cross Stitch (**X**), DMC color number (**DMC**), One-Quarter Stitch (**¼X**), Three-Quarter Stitch (**¾X**), Half Cross Stitch (**½X**), Backstitch (**B'ST**), J. & P. Coats color number (**JPC**), and color name (**COLOR**). Color key columns should be read vertically and horizontally to determine type of stitch and floss color.

STITCH DIAGRAMS

Counted Cross Stitch (X): Work one Cross Stitch to correspond to each colored square on the chart. For horizontal rows, work stitches in two journeys ***(Fig. 1)***. For vertical rows, complete each stitch as shown ***(Fig. 2)***. When the chart shows a Backstitch crossing a colored square ***(Fig. 3)***, a Cross Stitch ***(Fig. 1 or 2)*** should be worked first; then the Backstitch ***(Fig. 6)*** should be worked on top of the Cross Stitch.

Fig. 1

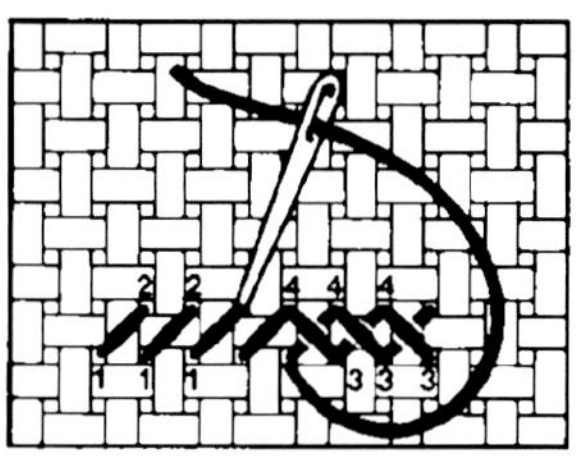

Fig. 2

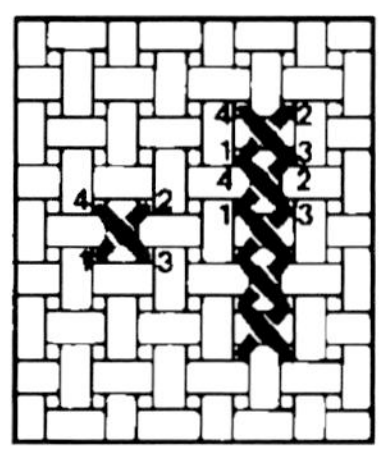

Fig. 3

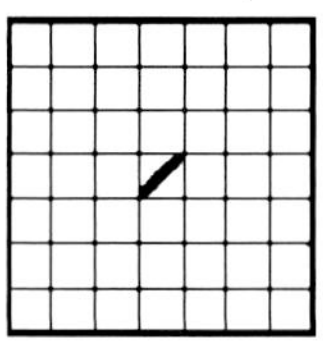

Half Cross Stitch (½X): This stitch is one journey of the Cross Stitch and is worked from lower left to upper right as shown in **Fig. 4**.

Fig. 4

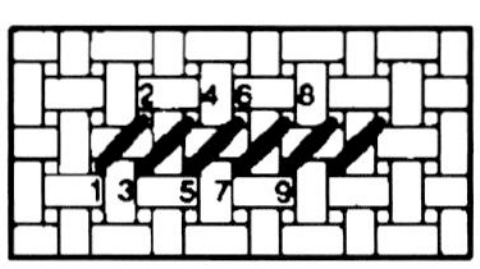

Quarter Stitch (¼X and ¾X): Quarter Stitches are denoted by triangular shapes of color on the chart and on the color key. Stitch 1-2 is the One-Quarter Stitch (¼X) ***(Fig. 5)***. When stitches 1-4 are worked in the same color, the resulting stitch is called a Three-Quarter Stitch (¾X).

Fig. 5

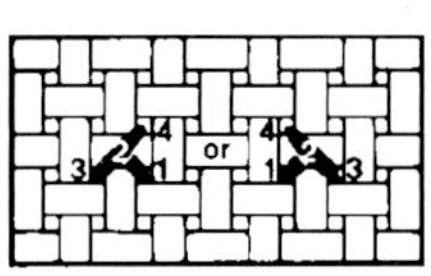

Backstitch (B'ST): For outline detail, Backstitch (shown on chart and on color key by colored straight lines) should be worked after the design has been completed ***(Fig. 6)***.

Fig. 6

FINISHING TECHNIQUE

STUFFED FIGURE FINISHING

Step 1. Cut a piece of Dirty Aida (14 ct) same size as stitched piece for backing.

Step 2. Matching right sides and raw edges and leaving bottom edge open, sew stitched piece and backing fabric together ⅛" from outer edges of design as shown in **Fig. 7**. Leaving a ¼" seam allowance, cut out figure. Clip seam allowances at curves; turn figure right side out and carefully push curves outward. Trim bottom edge of figure ½" from bottom of design. Press raw edges ¼" to wrong side; stuff figure with polyester fiberfill up to 1½" from opening.

Fig. 1

Step 3. For base, set figure on tracing paper and draw around base of figure. Add a ½" seam allowance to pattern; cut out. Place pattern on a piece of Dirty Aida. Use fabric marking pencil to draw around pattern; cut out along drawn line. Baste around base piece ½" from raw edge; press raw edges to wrong side along basting line.

Step 4. To weight bottom of figure, fill a plastic sandwich bag with a small amount of aquarium gravel. Place bag of gravel into opening of figure.

Step 5. Pin wrong side of base piece over opening. Whipstitch in place, adding polyester fiberfill as necessary to fill bottom of figure. Remove basting threads.

PROJECTS

Cover models were stitched on Dirty Aida (14 ct) using 3 strands of floss for Cross Stitch and 1 strand for Half Cross Stitch and Backstitch.